Diabetic Smoothies

Satisfying and Nutritious Smoothies for Balanced Blood Sugar

Jessica C. Hilton

Table of Contents

INTRODUCTION

Smoothies are a delicious and nutritious way to manage diabetes. By choosing the right ingredients, you can create a drink that not only tastes great but also helps control blood sugar levels. This book provides you with a comprehensive guide to making diabetic smoothies that are healthy and tasty.

Diabetes is a chronic disorder that affects millions of individuals globally. It is characterized by high blood sugar levels that can lead to a range of health problems, including heart disease, stroke, and kidney damage. While there is no cure for diabetes, it can be managed with a healthy diet, regular exercise, and medication.

Smoothies are an excellent addition to a diabetic diet because they are easy to make, convenient to consume, and can be packed with nutrient-dense ingredients. This book will show you how to create smoothies that are both delicious and nutritious, helping you manage your diabetes more effectively.

Benefits of Smoothies for Managing Diabetes

Smoothies are a popular and convenient way to consume fruits, vegetables, and other nutritious ingredients. For people with diabetes, incorporating smoothies into their diet can offer several benefits for managing their condition.

1. Control Blood Sugar Levels

Smoothies made with low-glycemic index (GI) ingredients can help regulate blood sugar levels. The glycemic index is a measure of how quickly carbohydrates in food are converted into glucose in the bloodstream. Foods with a high GI value can cause a rapid spike in blood sugar levels, which can be problematic for people with diabetes. On the other hand, foods with a low GI value are digested more slowly, resulting in a slower and more stable rise in blood sugar levels.

By choosing low-GI ingredients for their smoothies, people with diabetes can help maintain steady blood sugar levels throughout the day. Examples of low-GI ingredients include leafy greens, berries, avocado, nuts, and seeds.

2. Increase Nutrient Intake

Smoothies can be a great way to increase nutrient intake, especially for people who struggle to eat enough fruits and vegetables. By blending together a variety of ingredients, people with diabetes can easily consume a range of vitamins, minerals, and antioxidants.

Some nutrient-dense ingredients that can be added to diabetic smoothies include spinach, kale, broccoli, berries, chia seeds, flaxseed, and nuts. These ingredients can help improve overall health and reduce the risk of chronic diseases.

3. Boost Energy Levels

Diabetes can cause fluctuations in energy levels, and it's important for people with the condition to maintain stable energy throughout the day. Smoothies can be a good option for a quick and healthy energy boost. By including ingredients like bananas, berries, and Greek yogurt, people with diabetes can create smoothies that provide sustained energy without causing blood sugar spikes.

4. Aid in Weight Management

Maintaining a healthy weight is important for managing diabetes, and smoothies can be a useful tool in achieving this goal. Smoothies made with low-calorie, nutrient-dense ingredients can help people with diabetes feel full and satisfied without consuming excess calories. Additionally, smoothies can be used as a meal replacement for people who struggle with portion control or who have difficulty preparing meals.

Choosing the Right Ingredients for Diabetic Smoothies

Choosing the right ingredients for diabetic smoothies is crucial for managing blood sugar levels and overall health. Here are some tips for selecting ingredients for diabetic smoothies:

1. Choose Low-Glycemic Index (GI) Fruits

Fruits are a common ingredient in smoothies, but it's important to choose fruits with a low GI value to avoid blood sugar spikes. Some low-GI fruits that are suitable for diabetic smoothies include berries, apples, pears, and citrus fruits.

Avoid using high-GI fruits like watermelon, pineapple, and mango, which can cause rapid increases in blood sugar levels.

2. Add Leafy Greens

Leafy greens are packed with nutrients and are low in calories and carbohydrates, making them an excellent ingredient for diabetic smoothies. Spinach, kale, and collard greens are all terrific choices. Adding leafy greens to a smoothie can also help slow down the absorption of sugar into the bloodstream, reducing the impact on blood sugar levels.

3. Include Healthy Fats

Adding healthy fats to diabetic smoothies can help slow down the absorption of sugar into the bloodstream and promote satiety. Good sources of healthy fats include avocado, nuts, seeds, and nut butters.

It's important to use these ingredients in moderation, as they are high in calories. A small handful of nuts or a quarter of an avocado is usually sufficient.

4. Use Non-Dairy Milk

Dairy milk contains lactose, which is a form of sugar that can cause blood sugar spikes. Non-dairy milk alternatives like almond milk, coconut milk, or soy milk are lower in carbohydrates and can be a better option for diabetic smoothies.

5. Avoid Added Sugars

Many smoothie recipes call for added sugars like honey or maple syrup. These sweeteners can cause rapid increases in blood sugar levels and should be avoided in diabetic smoothies.

Instead, use natural sweeteners like stevia, a low-calorie, zero-carbohydrate sweetener made from the leaves of the stevia plant.

6. Consider Adding Protein

Adding protein to diabetic smoothies can help promote satiety and stabilize blood sugar levels. Good sources of protein include Greek yogurt, cottage cheese, and protein powder.

Be sure to choose protein powders that are low in sugar and carbohydrates, as some can be high in these ingredients.

Top 10 Superfoods for Diabetic Smoothies

Here are the top 10 superfoods for diabetic smoothies:

1. Leafy Greens

Leafy greens like spinach, kale, and Swiss chard are excellent choices for diabetic smoothies. They are low in carbohydrates and calories and rich in vitamins, minerals, and antioxidants. Leafy greens can help improve insulin sensitivity and reduce the risk of chronic diseases.

2. Berries

Berries like strawberries, blueberries, and raspberries are low in sugar and high in fiber, making them a great choice for diabetic smoothies. They are also rich in antioxidants, which can help reduce inflammation and protect against cell damage.

3. Avocado

Avocado is a nutrient-dense fruit that is strong in healthful fats and fiber.

It has a low glycemic index, which indicates it can help manage blood sugar levels. Avocado can also help improve cholesterol levels and reduce the risk of heart disease.

4. Greek Yogurt

Greek yogurt is a great source of protein and calcium, which can help improve blood sugar control and bone health. It is also low in carbohydrates and can help keep you feeling full and satisfied.

5. Chia Seeds

Chia seeds are high in fiber, omega-3 fatty acids, and antioxidants. They can help improve blood sugar control and reduce inflammation. Chia seeds can also help promote satiety and reduce appetite, making them a great addition to diabetic smoothies.

6. Cinnamon

Cinnamon has been demonstrated to boost insulin sensitivity and lower blood sugar levels. It also contains anti-inflammatory and antioxidant qualities, according to research. Adding a sprinkle of cinnamon to diabetic smoothies can provide both flavor and health benefits.

7. Flaxseed

Flaxseed is a great source of fiber and healthy fats, including omega-3 fatty acids. It has been shown to improve blood sugar control and reduce inflammation. Flaxseed can also help promote satiety and reduce appetite.

8. Nuts

Nuts such as almonds, walnuts, and pecans are high in protein, healthy fats, and fiber. They can aid in blood sugar regulation and lower the risk of heart disease. Nuts can also help promote satiety and reduce appetite.

9. Turmeric

Turmeric is a spice known for its anti-inflammatory and antioxidant qualities.

It has the potential to improve insulin sensitivity and lower the risk of chronic illnesses. Adding a pinch of turmeric to diabetic smoothies can provide both flavor and health benefits.

10. Coconut Oil

Coconut oil contains medium-chain triglycerides (MCTs), a form of healthful fat that may be rapidly turned into energy. It has been demonstrated to increase insulin sensitivity and decrease inflammation. Adding a small amount of coconut oil to diabetic smoothies can provide both flavor and health benefits.

The Recipes for Diabetic Smoothies

1. Spinach and Avocado Smoothie

Preparation Time: 10 minutes

Yield: 2 servings

Ingredients:

- 1 ripe avocado
- 2 cups baby spinach
- 1 medium-sized green apple
- 1/2 cup unsweetened almond milk
- 1/2 cup ice
- 1 tablespoon chia seeds
- 1/2 teaspoon ground cinnamon

Directions

1. Cut the avocado in half, remove the pit, and scoop out the flesh into a blender.
2. Add the baby spinach, green apple, almond milk, ice, chia seeds, and ground cinnamon to the blender.
3. Combine all of the ingredients in a blender and blend until smooth and creamy.
4. Immediately pour the smoothie into a glass and serve.

Nutritional Information per Serving:

- Calories: 215
- Total Fat: 13g
- Saturated Fat: 2g
- Sodium: 94mg
- Total Carbohydrate: 26g
- Dietary Fiber: 12g
- Sugars: 11g
- Protein: 4g

2. Kale and Apple Smoothie

Preparation time: 10 minutes

Yield: 1 serving

Ingredients:

- 1 cup kale, chopped
- 1 medium apple, cored and chopped
- 1/2 medium avocado, pitted and peeled
- 1/2 cup unsweetened almond milk
- 1/4 teaspoon ground cinnamon
- 1 tablespoon chia seeds
- 1/2 cup ice cubes

Directions:

1. In a blender, combine the chopped kale, chopped apple, peeled avocado, unsweetened almond milk, ground cinnamon, chia seeds, and ice cubes.
2. Blend on high speed until smooth, about 30-45 seconds.
3. Taste and adjust the sweetness by adding a small amount of stevia or another low-calorie sweetener if needed.

4. Pour into a glass and enjoy!

Nutritional Information per serving:

- Calories: 304
- Total Fat: 17g
- Saturated Fat: 2g
- Sodium: 104mg
- Total Carbohydrates: 36g
- Dietary Fiber: 14g
- Sugars: 16g
- Protein: 6g

3. Cucumber and Celery Smoothie

Preparation time: 10 minutes

Yield: 2 servings

Ingredients:

- 1 medium cucumber, chopped
- 2 stalks of celery, chopped
- 1 small green apple, that has been peeled and cut into small pieces
- 1/2 cup of spinach leaves
- 1/2 cup of unsweetened almond milk
- 1/2 cup of water
- 1/2 teaspoon of ground cinnamon
- 1/2 teaspoon of grated ginger
- 1 tablespoon of lemon juice
- 1 tablespoon of chia seeds

Directions:

1. Add the chopped cucumber, celery, apple, and spinach leaves into a blender.
2. Pour in the almond milk and water.
3. Add the cinnamon, grated ginger, and lemon juice.
4. Blend until smooth.
5. Incorporate the chia seeds into the mixture by pulsing until thoroughly blended.
6. Pour into a glass and serve.

Nutritional information per serving:

- Calories: 102
- Total fat: 3.6g
- Saturated fat: 0.3g
- Sodium: 83mg
- Total carbohydrates: 18.5g
- Dietary fiber: 6.8g
- Sugar: 8.6g
- Protein: 3.2g

4. Broccoli and Pear Smoothie

Preparation Time: 10 minutes

Yield: 2 servings

Ingredients:

- 1 cup of broccoli florets, either fresh or frozen.
- 1 ripe pear, cored and chopped
- 1 small banana, peeled
- 1/2 cup unsweetened almond milk
- 1/2 teaspoon ground cinnamon
- 1/2 cup ice cubes

Directions:

1. In a blender, combine the broccoli, pear, banana, almond milk, and cinnamon. Blend until smooth.
2. Add the ice cubes and blend again until the smoothie reaches your desired consistency.
3. Taste and adjust sweetness, if necessary.
4. Pour into glasses and serve immediately.

Nutritional Information per Serving:

- Calories: 110
- Total Fat: 0.5g
- Sodium: 40mg
- Total Carbohydrates: 27g
- Dietary Fiber: 7g
- Sugars: 13g
- Protein: 4g

5. Ginger and Cucumber Smoothie

Preparation time: 10 minutes

Yield: 1 serving

<u>Ingredients:</u>

- 1 medium cucumber, chopped
- 1 fresh ginger, approximately 1 inch in size, peeled and finely chopped.
- 1 cup unsweetened almond milk
- 1/2 avocado
- 1/2 tsp. vanilla extract

- 1 tsp. honey (optional)
- Ice cubes (optional)

Directions:

1. Add the chopped cucumber and ginger to a blender and blend until smooth.
2. Add the almond milk, avocado, vanilla extract, and honey (if using) to the blender and blend again until smooth.
3. If desired, add ice cubes to the blender and blend until smooth.
4. Transfer the smoothie into a glass and serve promptly

Nutritional information per serving:

- Calories: 197
- Fat: 15g
- Saturated Fat: 2g
- Sodium: 141mg
- Carbohydrates: 14g
- Fiber: 8g
- Sugar: 4g

- Protein: 4g

6. Berry Blast Smoothie

Preparation time: 5 minutes

Yield: 1 serving

Ingredients:

- 1 cup of frozen berries, comprising a combination of strawberries, raspberries, and blueberries.
- 1 small banana
- 1 cup unsweetened almond milk
- 1/2 cup plain Greek yogurt
- 1 tsp vanilla extract
- 1 tbsp chia seeds
- 1/4 tsp cinnamon
- 1 packet stevia (optional)
- Ice cubes (optional)

Directions:

1. In a blender, combine all the ingredients except for the ice cubes.

2. Blend on a high speed until the mixture becomes smooth and creamy.
3. Taste the mixture and adjust sweetness to your liking by adding stevia if necessary.
4. Add ice cubes if you'd like your smoothie to be colder and thicker.
5. Blend again until the ice cubes are fully incorporated.
6. Transfer the smoothie into a glass and promptly serve.

Nutritional information per serving:

- Calories: 220
- Total fat: 5g
- Saturated fat: 1g
- Cholesterol: 5mg
- Sodium: 160mg
- Total carbohydrates: 35g
- Dietary fiber: 9g
- Sugars: 17g
- Protein: 12g

7. Mango and Banana Smoothie

Preparation time: 10 minutes

Yield: 2 servings

Ingredients:

- 1 ripe mango, peeled and chopped
- 1 ripe banana, peeled and sliced
- 1 cup unsweetened almond milk
- 1/2 teaspoon vanilla extract
- 1/2 teaspoon ground cinnamon
- 1 tablespoon chia seeds
- 1 cup ice cubes

Directions:

1. In a blender, combine the chopped mango, sliced banana, almond milk, vanilla extract, and ground cinnamon.
2. Blend on a high speed until the mixture becomes smooth and creamy.
3. Add the chia seeds and blend for another 10-15 seconds.

4. Add the ice cubes and blend again until the smoothie is thick and frosty.
5. Taste and adjust the sweetness if necessary.
6. Pour into glasses and serve immediately.

Nutritional information per serving:

- Calories: 170
- Total fat: 4g
- Sodium: 80mg
- Total carbohydrates: 32g
- Dietary fiber: 7g
- Sugars: 18g
- Protein: 3g

8. Pineapple and Coconut Smoothie

Preparation Time: 5 minutes

Yield: 2 servings

Ingredients:

- 2 cups fresh pineapple chunks

- 1 cup coconut milk
- 1/2 cup ice cubes
- 1/2 teaspoon vanilla extract
- 1 teaspoon honey (optional)

Directions:

1. Add the pineapple chunks, coconut milk, ice cubes, vanilla extract, and honey (if using) to a blender.
2. Blend on high speed for 1-2 minutes until the ingredients are well combined and the smoothie is creamy.
3. Taste and adjust sweetness with more honey, if desired.
4. Pour the smoothie into glasses and serve immediately.

Nutritional Information per Serving:

- Calories: 160
- Total Fat: 4g
- Saturated Fat: 3g
- Sodium: 9mg
- Total Carbohydrate: 34g

- Dietary Fiber: 3g
- Sugars: 24g
- Protein: 1g

9. Strawberry and Kiwi Smoothie

Preparation Time: 10 minutes

Yield: 2 servings

<u>Ingredients:</u>

- 1 cup frozen strawberries
- 1 kiwi, peeled and chopped
- 1/2 cup unsweetened almond milk
- 1/2 cup plain Greek yogurt
- 1/2 teaspoon vanilla extract
- 1 teaspoon honey (optional)
- 1/2 cup ice cubes

Directions:

1. In a blender, add frozen strawberries, chopped kiwi, almond milk, Greek yogurt, vanilla extract, and honey (if using).
2. Blend the ingredients until smooth.
3. Include ice cubes and blend once more until achieving a smooth consistency.
4. Taste the smoothie and adjust the sweetness as desired by adding more honey or a sugar substitute.
5. Transfer the smoothie into a glass and promptly serve.

Nutritional Information per Serving:

- Calories: 107
- Total Fat: 2g
- Cholesterol: 4mg
- Sodium: 72mg
- Total Carbohydrates: 15g
- Dietary Fiber: 3g
- Sugars: 9g
- Protein: 9g

10. Papaya and Lime Smoothie

Preparation time: 10 minutes

Yield: 2 servings

Ingredients:

- 1 small papaya, peeled and seeded
- Juice of 1 lime
- 1/2 cup plain Greek yogurt
- 1/2 cup unsweetened almond milk
- 1 teaspoon honey (optional)
- 1/2 teaspoon vanilla extract
- 1 cup ice cubes

Directions:

1. Cut the papaya into small chunks and add them to a blender.
2. Add the lime juice, Greek yogurt, almond milk, honey (if using), and vanilla extract to the blender.
3. Add the ice cubes to the blender and blend everything together until smooth and creamy.

4. Transfer the smoothie into a glass and promptly serve.

Nutritional information per serving:

- Calories: 135
- Total fat: 3g
- Saturated fat: 0.5g
- Cholesterol: 5mg
- Sodium: 80mg
- Total carbohydrate: 23g
- Dietary fiber: 3g
- Total sugars: 16g
- Protein: 7g

11. Peanut Butter and Banana Smoothie

Preparation time: 5 minutes

Yield: 1 serving

<u>Ingredients:</u>

- 1 ripe banana

- 2 tablespoons of natural peanut butter (without added sugar)
- 1 cup unsweetened almond milk (or any other unsweetened milk of your choice)
- 1/2 teaspoon cinnamon powder
- 1/2 teaspoon vanilla extract
- 1/2 cup of ice cubes

Directions:

1. Peel the banana and slice it into bite-sized chunks.
2. Add the banana, peanut butter, almond milk, cinnamon powder, vanilla extract, and ice cubes to a blender.
3. Blend the ingredients until the smoothie is smooth and creamy.
4. Transfer the smoothie into a glass and promptly serve.

Nutritional information per serving:

- Calories: 275
- Total Fat: 16 g
- Saturated Fat: 2.5 g

- Sodium: 160 mg
- Total Carbohydrates: 27 g
- Dietary Fiber: 6 g
- Total Sugars: 10 g
- Protein: 9 g

12. Almond Butter and Mixed Berries Smoothie

Preparation Time: 5 minutes

Yield: 1 serving

<u>Ingredients:</u>

- 1 cup mixed berries (fresh or frozen)
- 1 banana, sliced
- 1 tablespoon almond butter
- 1/2 cup unsweetened almond milk
- 1/2 teaspoon ground cinnamon
- 1/2 teaspoon vanilla extract
- 1/2 cup ice cubes

Directions:

1. In a blender, combine mixed berries, banana, almond butter, unsweetened almond milk, ground cinnamon, and vanilla extract.
2. Blend at a high speed until the mixture becomes velvety and smooth.
3. Add ice cubes and blend again until the mixture is thick and smooth.
4. Transfer the smoothie into a glass and promptly serve.

Nutritional Information per Serving:

- Calories: 220
- Total Fat: 9g
- Saturated Fat: 1g
- Sodium: 130mg
- Total Carbohydrates: 34g
- Dietary Fiber: 7g
- Sugars: 18g
- Protein: 5g

13. Vanilla Protein Powder and Raspberry Smoothie

Preparation Time: 5 minutes

Yield: 1 serving

Ingredients:

- 1/2 cup frozen raspberries
- 1 scoop vanilla protein powder (sugar-free)
- 1/2 cup unsweetened almond milk
- 1/4 cup plain Greek yogurt
- 1/2 teaspoon vanilla extract
- 1/2 teaspoon cinnamon
- 1/2 teaspoon stevia (optional)
- 1/2 cup ice cubes

Directions:

1. Combine all ingredients in a blender.
2. Blend on high speed for about 30 seconds or until smooth and creamy.
3. Transfer the smoothie into a glass and promptly serve.

Nutritional Information per Serving:

- Calories: 185
- Fat: 4g
- Carbohydrates: 15g
- Fiber: 5g
- Protein: 25g

14. Chocolate Protein Powder and Almond Milk Smoothie

Preparation time: 5 minutes

Yield: 1 serving

<u>Ingredients:</u>

- 1 scoop chocolate protein powder (look for a brand that is low in sugar and carbohydrates)
- 1 cup unsweetened almond milk
- 1/2 medium avocado
- 1 tablespoon unsweetened cocoa powder
- 1/2 teaspoon vanilla extract
- 1 cup ice

Directions:

1. Combine all the ingredients in a blender and blend until a smooth consistency is achieved.
2. If the smoothie is too thick, add a bit more almond milk to thin it out.
3. Pour into a glass and enjoy immediately.

Nutritional information per serving:

- Calories: 290
- Total fat: 16g
- Saturated fat: 2g
- Sodium: 250mg
- Total carbohydrates: 14g
- Dietary fiber: 8g
- Sugars: 2g
- Protein: 23g

15. Chocolate and Banana Smoothie

Preparation Time: 5 minutes

Yield: 1 serving

Ingredients:

- 1 ripe banana, sliced
- 1 tablespoon unsweetened cocoa powder
- 1/2 cup plain, unsweetened Greek yogurt
- 1/2 cup unsweetened almond milk
- 1/2 teaspoon vanilla extract
- 1 teaspoon honey (optional)
- 1 cup ice

Directions:

1. Put all the ingredients into a blender.
2. Combine the ingredients and blend until the mixture reaches a smooth consistency.
3. Pour into a glass and serve.

Nutritional Information (per serving):

- Calories: 180
- Total Fat: 4g
- Saturated Fat: 1.5g
- Cholesterol: 5mg
- Sodium: 130mg
- Total Carbohydrates: 28g
- Dietary Fiber: 4g
- Sugars: 14g
- Protein: 12g

16. Vanilla and Blueberry Smoothie

Preparation Time: 5 minutes

Yield: 1 serving

<u>Ingredients:</u>

- 1/2 cup frozen blueberries
- 1/2 cup unsweetened almond milk
- 1/2 tsp vanilla extract
- 1/4 cup plain Greek yogurt

- 1 tsp ground flaxseed

Directions:

1. In a blender, add frozen blueberries, almond milk, vanilla extract, Greek yogurt, ground flaxseed, and honey (if using).
2. Blend until smooth and creamy.
3. If the mixture is too thick, add a little more almond milk to thin it out.
4. Taste and adjust sweetness if necessary.
5. Serve immediately and enjoy!

Nutritional Information (per serving):

- Calories: 150
- Fat: 5g
- Carbohydrates: 17g
- Fiber: 3g
- Protein: 9g
- Sugar: 11g

17. Coffee and Almond Smoothie

Preparation time: 5 minutes

Yield: 1 serving

Ingredients:

- 1 cup unsweetened almond milk
- 1/2 cup brewed coffee, cooled
- 1/2 ripe banana
- 1/4 cup almond butter
- 1 tsp vanilla extract
- 1/2 tsp ground cinnamon
- 1/2 tsp stevia or other sugar substitute (optional)
- 1 cup ice cubes

Directions:

1. In a blender, combine the almond milk, coffee, banana, almond butter, vanilla extract, cinnamon, and stevia (if using).
2. Incorporate the ice cubes and blend until a smooth consistency is achieved.

3. Transfer the smoothie into a glass and savor its deliciousness

Nutritional information per serving:

- Calories: 288
- Total Fat: 20g
- Saturated Fat: 1.5g
- Sodium: 185mg
- Total Carbohydrates: 22g
- Dietary Fiber: 6g
- Sugars: 9g
- Protein: 8g

18. Cherry and Chocolate Smoothie

Preparation time: 5 minutes

Yield: 1 serving

<u>Ingredients:</u>

- 1 cup unsweetened almond milk
- 1/2 cup frozen cherries

- 1/4 avocado
- 1 tbsp unsweetened cocoa powder
- 1 tsp honey or stevia (optional)
- 1 scoop vanilla protein powder (optional)

Directions:

1. Add almond milk, frozen cherries, avocado, cocoa powder, and honey or stevia (if using) to a blender.
2. Blend until smooth and creamy.
3. If you'd like, you can include a serving of vanilla protein powder and blend once more until the mixture becomes smooth.
4. Pour into a glass and serve immediately.

Nutritional information per serving:

- Calories: 220
- Total fat: 11g
- Saturated fat: 1.5g
- Sodium: 160mg
- Total carbohydrates: 21g
- Dietary fiber: 6g
- Sugars: 11g

- Protein: 14g

19. Green Goddess Smoothie

Yield: 1 large serving.

Ingredients:

- 1 cup unsweetened almond milk
- 1/2 ripe avocado
- 1 cup fresh spinach
- 1/2 cup fresh parsley
- 1/2 cup fresh mint leaves
- 1/2 cup chopped cucumber
- 1/2 tsp grated ginger
- 1/4 tsp ground cinnamon
- 1/2 tsp vanilla extract
- 1 tbsp chia seeds
- 1 scoop unflavored protein powder (optional)
- Ice cubes as needed

Directions:

1. In a blender, add the almond milk, avocado, spinach, parsley, mint leaves, cucumber, ginger, cinnamon, and vanilla extract. Blend until smooth.

2. Add the chia seeds and protein powder (if using) and blend again until smooth.

3. In case the smoothie has a thicker texture than desired, include a few ice cubes and blend once more until the desired consistency is achieved.

4. Pour into a glass and enjoy!

Nutritional information per serving:

- Calories: 321
- Total Fat: 21g
- Saturated Fat: 3g
- Sodium: 202mg
- Total Carbohydrates: 21g
- Dietary Fiber: 12g
- Sugars: 3g
- Protein: 20g

20. Apple Pie Smoothie

Preparation time: 5 minutes

Yield: 1 serving

Ingredients:

- 1 medium apple, peeled and chopped
- 1/2 cup plain non-fat Greek yogurt
- 1/4 cup unsweetened almond milk
- 1/4 teaspoon ground cinnamon
- 1/4 teaspoon vanilla extract
- 1/4 teaspoon ground nutmeg
- 1 cup ice cubes

Directions:

1. In a blender, combine the chopped apple, Greek yogurt, almond milk, cinnamon, vanilla extract, nutmeg, and ice cubes.
2. Blend until smooth and creamy.
3. Transfer the smoothie to a glass and serve promptly.

Nutritional information per serving:

- Calories: 175
- Total fat: 0.5 g
- Sodium: 79 mg
- Total carbohydrates: 30 g
- Dietary fiber: 5 g
- Sugar: 21 g
- Protein: 14 g

21. Tropical Sunrise Smoothie

Preparation time: 5 minutes

Yield: 1 serving

Ingredients:

- 1 cup of unsweetened almond milk
- 1/2 cup of frozen pineapple chunks
- 1/2 cup of frozen mango chunks
- 1 small ripe banana
- 1 tbsp of chia seeds
- 1 tsp of grated ginger
- 1 tsp of vanilla extract

- 1 tsp of honey (optional)

Directions:

1. Place all the ingredients into a blender and blend until a smooth consistency is achieved
2. If the smoothie is too thick, you can add additional almond milk to reach the desired consistency.
3. Pour the smoothie into a glass and enjoy immediately.

Nutritional information per serving:

- Calories: 320
- Fat: 9g
- Carbohydrates: 57g
- Fiber: 11g
- Protein: 5g
- Sugar: 32g

22. Pumpkin Spice Smoothie

Preparation time: 5 minutes

Yield: 1 serving

Ingredients:

- 1/2 cup canned pumpkin puree (make sure it's unsweetened)
- 1/2 medium banana
- 1/2 cup unsweetened almond milk
- 1/2 teaspoon vanilla extract
- 1/2 teaspoon pumpkin pie spice
- 1/2 teaspoon cinnamon
- 1 scoop vanilla protein powder (optional)
- 1/2 cup ice cubes

Directions:

1. In a blender, combine the pumpkin puree, banana, almond milk, vanilla extract, pumpkin pie spice, cinnamon, and protein powder (if using).
2. Blend at a high speed until the mixture becomes smooth and creamy.

3. Add the ice cubes and blend again until the smoothie is thick and frosty.
4. Taste and adjust the spices to your liking.
5. Transfer the smoothie into a glass and serve promptly.

Nutritional information per serving:

- Calories: 170
- Total fat: 3.5g
- Saturated fat: 0.5g
- Cholesterol: 5mg
- Sodium: 135mg
- Total carbohydrates: 24g
- Dietary fiber: 7g
- Sugars: 10g
- Protein: 15g

23. Red Velvet Smoothie

Preparation Time: 10 minutes

Yield: 1 serving

Ingredients:

- 1 small beet, peeled and chopped
- 1/2 cup frozen strawberries
- 1/4 cup unsweetened almond milk
- 1/4 cup plain Greek yogurt
- 1 tablespoon cocoa powder
- 1 teaspoon vanilla extract
- 1/2 teaspoon cinnamon
- 1/2 teaspoon stevia (or your preferred sweetener)
- Ice cubes as needed

Directions:

1. Add the chopped beet, frozen strawberries, almond milk, Greek yogurt, cocoa powder, vanilla extract, cinnamon, and stevia to a blender.

2. Use a high-speed blender to thoroughly blend the ingredients until they become smooth, incorporating ice cubes as necessary to attain your preferred texture.

3. Transfer the smoothie into a glass and savor the deliciousness

Nutritional Information per serving:

- Calories: 178
- Total Fat: 4.4g
- Saturated Fat: 1.1g
- Cholesterol: 5mg
- Sodium: 164mg
- Total Carbohydrates: 27.6g
- Dietary Fiber: 6.4g
- Total Sugars: 16.6g
- Protein: 10.3g

24. Peach and Carrot Smoothie

Ingredients:

- 2 ripe peaches, peeled and pitted
- 1 large carrot, peeled and chopped
- 1/2 cup unsweetened almond milk
- 1/4 cup plain Greek yogurt
- 1 tsp honey (optional)
- 1 tsp grated fresh ginger (optional)
- 1 cup ice cubes

Directions:

1. In a blender, combine the peaches, carrot, almond milk, Greek yogurt, honey, and ginger (if using).
2. Blend the ingredients until smooth and well combined.
3. Add the ice cubes and blend again until the smoothie is thick and frosty.
4. Taste and adjust sweetness as desired, adding more honey if necessary.
5. Transfer the smoothie into a glass and serve promptly.

Nutritional information per serving:

- Calories: 110
- Total Fat: 2g
- Saturated Fat: 0.5g
- Cholesterol: 3mg
- Sodium: 77mg
- Total Carbohydrates: 22g
- Dietary Fiber: 3g
- Sugar: 17g
- Protein: 4g

25. Mango Ginger Smoothie

Preparation time: 5 minutes

Yield: 1 serving

Ingredients:

- Use 1 cup of diced mango, which can be either fresh or frozen.
- Take a fresh ginger root that measures 1/2 inch in diameter. Peel the skin off using a knife or a peeler, then grate the ginger finely using a grater or a zester.
- 1 cup unsweetened almond milk
- 1/4 cup plain Greek yogurt
- 1 tablespoon chia seeds
- 1 teaspoon vanilla extract
- 1-2 packets of stevia (optional)
- Ice cubes (optional)

Directions:

1. Add diced mango, grated ginger, almond milk, Greek yogurt, chia seeds, vanilla extract, and stevia (if using) into a blender.
2. Blend all the ingredients until smooth and creamy.
3. If the smoothie is too thick, add some ice cubes and blend again until desired consistency is achieved.
4. Transfer the smoothie to a glass and serve it cold.

Nutritional information per serving:

- Calories: 220
- Carbohydrates: 32g
- Protein: 9g
- Fat: 6g
- Fiber: 7g
- Sugar: 23g
- Sodium: 160mg

26. Apple Mint Avocado Smoothie

Preparation time: 10 minutes

Yield: 2 servings

Ingredients:

- 1 medium apple, cored and chopped
- 1 small avocado, pitted and peeled
- 1 cup fresh mint leaves
- 1 cup unsweetened almond milk
- 1 tablespoon chia seeds
- 1 teaspoon honey (optional)

Directions:

1. Add the chopped apple, avocado, mint leaves, almond milk, chia seeds, and honey (if using) to a blender.
2. Blend together the components until they become smooth and creamy.
3. Transfer the smoothie into a glass and serve promptly.

Nutritional information per serving:

- Calories: 214
- Total Fat: 14g
- Saturated Fat: 2g
- Sodium: 86mg
- Total Carbohydrates: 22g
- Dietary Fiber: 9g
- Sugars: 11g
- Protein: 4g

27. Banana Oatmeal Smoothie

Preparation time: 5 minutes

Yield: 1 serving

Ingredients:

- 1 medium-sized ripe banana
- 1/2 cup rolled oats
- 1/2 cup unsweetened almond milk
- 1/2 cup plain Greek yogurt
- 1 tsp ground cinnamon
- 1 tsp pure vanilla extract

- 1/2 cup ice cubes

Directions:

1. In a blender, add the ripe banana, rolled oats, almond milk, Greek yogurt, ground cinnamon, and pure vanilla extract.
2. Continuously blend the mixture until it achieves a smooth and creamy consistency.
3. Add the ice cubes and blend the mixture again until the ice is completely crushed and the smoothie has a thick consistency.
4. Transfer the smoothie into a glass and serve promptly.

Nutritional information per serving:

- Calories: 310
- Total Fat: 6g
- Saturated Fat: 1g
- Cholesterol: 5mg
- Sodium: 118mg
- Total Carbohydrates: 53g
- Dietary Fiber: 8g

- Sugars: 17g
- Protein: 17g

28. Blueberry Almond Smoothie

Preparation time: 5-10 minutes

Yield: 1 serving

Ingredients:

- 1 cup fresh or frozen blueberries
- 1 ripe banana
- 1/4 cup unsweetened almond milk
- 1/4 cup plain Greek yogurt
- 1/4 cup unsalted almonds
- 1 tsp vanilla extract
- 1 cup ice cubes

Directions:

1. In a blender, add blueberries, banana, almond milk, Greek yogurt, almonds, vanilla extract, and honey (if using).
2. Blend at a high speed until the mixture becomes smooth and creamy.

3. Incorporate ice cubes into the mixture and blend once more until the smoothie achieves the desired texture.

4. Taste the smoothie and adjust the sweetness by adding more honey if needed.

5. Transfer the smoothie into a glass and serve promptly.

Nutritional information per serving:

- Calories: 310
- Total Fat: 12g
- Saturated Fat: 1g
- Cholesterol: 5mg
- Sodium: 65mg
- Total Carbohydrates: 41g
- Dietary Fiber: 8g
- Total Sugars: 24g
- Protein: 13g

29. Strawberry Tofu Smoothie

Preparation time: 5 minutes

Yield: 1 serving

Ingredients:

- 1 cup fresh or frozen strawberries
- 1/2 cup silken tofu
- 1/2 cup unsweetened almond milk
- 1/2 tsp vanilla extract
- 1-2 tsp honey or stevia to taste (optional)
- Ice cubes (optional)

Directions:

1. Wash and remove the stems of the strawberries, and chop them into smaller pieces if necessary.
2. In a blender, add the strawberries, silken tofu, almond milk, vanilla extract, and sweetener if using.
3. Blend at a high speed for 30 to 60 seconds, or until the mixture achieves a smooth and creamy consistency.

4. If you prefer a thicker smoothie, add a few ice cubes and blend again until smooth.

5. Transfer the smoothie into a glass and serve promptly.

Nutritional information per serving:

- Calories: 150
- Total Fat: 4g
- Sodium: 75mg
- Total Carbohydrates: 22g
- Dietary Fiber: 4g
- Sugars: 13g
- Protein: 9g

30. Cucumber Pineapple Smoothie

Preparation Time: 10 minutes

Yield: 2 servings

Ingredients:

- 1 cup chopped fresh pineapple
- 1/2 medium cucumber, peeled and chopped
- 1/2 cup unsweetened almond milk
- 1/2 cup plain Greek yogurt
- 1 tablespoon fresh lime juice
- 1/2 teaspoon grated fresh ginger
- 1 cup ice cubes

Directions:

1. Add the pineapple, cucumber, almond milk, Greek yogurt, lime juice, and ginger to a blender.
2. Blend on high speed until the ingredients are well combined and smooth.
3. Add the ice cubes and blend again until the smoothie is thick and frosty.

4. Taste and adjust the sweetness, if necessary, by adding a natural sweetener like stevia or honey.

5. Transfer the smoothie into a glass and serve promptly.

Nutritional Information per Serving:

- Calories: 125
- Total Fat: 2.8g
- Saturated Fat: 0.2g
- Cholesterol: 2mg
- Sodium: 68mg
- Total Carbohydrates: 19.9g
- Dietary Fiber: 2.5g
- Sugars: 13.5g
- Protein: 8.2g

31. Frozen Banana Smoothie

Preparation time: 5 minutes

Yield: 2 servings

Ingredients:

- 2 ripe bananas, peeled and sliced
- 1 cup unsweetened almond milk
- 1/2 cup plain Greek yogurt
- 1 tablespoon honey (or other natural sweetener like stevia or monk fruit)
- 1/2 teaspoon ground cinnamon
- 1/2 teaspoon vanilla extract
- 2 cups ice

Directions:

1. Add the sliced bananas, almond milk, Greek yogurt, honey, cinnamon, and vanilla extract to a blender. Blend until smooth.
2. Add the ice and blend again until the mixture is smooth and creamy.

3. Transfer the smoothie into a glass and serve promptly.

Nutritional information per serving:

- Calories: 174
- Total fat: 3g
- Saturated fat: 1g
- Cholesterol: 4mg
- Sodium: 90mg
- Total carbohydrates: 33g
- Dietary fiber: 3g
- Sugars: 20g
- Protein: 6g

32. Cinnamon Roll Smoothie

Preparation time: 5 minutes

Yield: 1 serving

Ingredients:

- 1 cup unsweetened almond milk
- 1/2 cup plain Greek yogurt
- 1/2 cup cauliflower florets

- 1/2 banana, frozen
- 1/2 tsp vanilla extract
- 1 tsp ground cinnamon
- 1 tbsp almond butter
- 1 tbsp ground flaxseed
- 1/2 scoop vanilla protein powder
- 1/2 cup ice cubes

Directions:

1. Combine all the ingredients in a blender and blend until they form a smooth and creamy mixture.
2. Adjust sweetness with stevia, if desired.
3. Serve in a glass and enjoy!

Nutritional information per serving:

- Calories: 300
- Total fat: 15g
- Saturated fat: 1.5g
- Cholesterol: 10mg
- Sodium: 250mg
- Total carbohydrates: 22g
- Dietary fiber: 8g

- Sugars: 7g
- Protein: 24g

33. Pineapple Banana Shake

Preparation time: 10 minutes

Yield: 2 servings

Ingredients:

- 1 cup fresh pineapple chunks
- 1 medium banana
- 1 cup unsweetened almond milk
- 1/2 teaspoon vanilla extract
- 1/2 teaspoon ground cinnamon
- 1 cup ice cubes

Directions:

1. First, peel the banana and cut it into small chunks.
2. Cut the pineapple into chunks.
3. Add the banana, pineapple, almond milk, vanilla extract, and cinnamon to a blender.
4. Blend the ingredients at a high speed until they are smooth and creamy.

5. Add the ice cubes and blend again until the shake is thick and frothy.

6. Pour the shake into a glass and serve immediately.

Nutritional information per serving:

- Calories: 99
- Total fat: 2g
- Sodium: 89mg
- Total carbohydrates: 22g
- Dietary fiber: 3g
- Sugars: 12g
- Protein: 2g

34. Coconut Milk Strawberry Smoothie

Preparation Time: 5 minutes

Yield: 1 serving

<u>Ingredients:</u>

- 1 cup unsweetened coconut milk
- 1 cup frozen strawberries

- 1 tablespoon chia seeds
- 1 teaspoon vanilla extract
- 1 teaspoon honey (optional)

Directions:

1. Add the coconut milk, frozen strawberries, chia seeds, vanilla extract, and honey (if using) into a blender.
2. Blend the combination until it is smooth and creamy
3. Transfer the smoothie into a glass and serve promptly.

Nutritional Information per serving:

- Calories: 208
- Total Fat: 14g
- Saturated Fat: 10g
- Sodium: 25mg
- Total Carbohydrates: 20g
- Dietary Fiber: 6g
- Sugars: 10g
- Protein: 3g

35. Key Lime Pie Protein Shake Smoothie

Preparation time: 5 minutes

Yield: 1 serving

Ingredients:

- 1 cup unsweetened almond milk
- 1 scoop vanilla protein powder
- 1/2 cup plain Greek yogurt
- 1 tbsp lime juice
- 1 tsp lime zest
- 1/2 tsp vanilla extract
- 1/4 tsp cinnamon
- 1/4 avocado, diced
- 1 cup ice cubes
- Whipped cream and additional lime zest for garnish (optional)

Directions:

1. In a blender, combine the almond milk, protein powder, Greek yogurt, lime juice, lime zest, vanilla extract, cinnamon, and avocado.
2. Blend until smooth.
3. Add the ice cubes and blend until the mixture is creamy and frothy.
4. Pour the shake into a glass and top with whipped cream and additional lime zest, if desired.
5. Enjoy immediately.

Nutritional information per serving:

- Calories: 293
- Fat: 10g
- Carbohydrates: 15g
- Fiber: 5g
- Protein: 33g

36. Vegan Blueberry Smoothie

Preparation time: 5 minutes

Yield: 2 servings

Ingredients:

- 1 cup frozen blueberries
- 1 medium banana
- 1/2 cup unsweetened almond milk
- 1/2 cup plain Greek yogurt (vegan option: use soy or coconut yogurt)
- 1 tablespoon ground flaxseed
- 1/4 teaspoon cinnamon
- 1/4 teaspoon vanilla extract
- 1/2 cup ice cubes (optional)

Directions:

1. Place all the ingredients into a blender and blend until a smooth consistency is achieved. If the mixture appears excessively thick, incorporate additional almond milk or water to achieve a thinner texture.

2. Taste and adjust the sweetness by adding a little stevia, if desired.
3. Transfer the smoothie into a glass and serve promptly.

Nutritional information per serving:

- Calories: 132
- Total Fat: 3.1g
- Saturated Fat: 0.4g
- Sodium: 45mg
- Total Carbohydrates: 23.3g
- Dietary Fiber: 4.6g
- Total Sugars: 12.6g
- Protein: 5.9g

37. Coconut Chia Spinach Smoothie

Preparation time: 5 minutes

Yield: 1 serving

Ingredients:

- 1 cup unsweetened coconut milk
- 1/2 cup fresh spinach leaves
- 1 tablespoon chia seeds
- 1/2 teaspoon vanilla extract
- 1/4 teaspoon ground cinnamon
- 1/2 cup ice cubes

Directions:

1. Add the coconut milk, spinach, chia seeds, vanilla extract, and cinnamon to a blender.
2. Blend the ingredients at a high speed until they become smooth and creamy.
3. Add the ice cubes and blend again until the ice is fully incorporated and the smoothie is thick and frosty.

4. Transfer the smoothie into a glass and savor the delightful blend!

Nutritional information per serving:

- Calories: 179
- Total fat: 12g
- Saturated fat: 10g
- Sodium: 23mg
- Total carbohydrates: 15g
- Dietary fiber: 8g
- Total sugars: 1g
- Protein: 3g

38. Carrot Smoothie

Preparation time: 10 minutes

Yield: 2 servings

<u>Ingredients:</u>

- 2 medium-sized carrots, peeled and chopped
- 1 medium-sized apple, peeled and chopped
- 1 cup of unsweetened almond milk
- 1 tablespoon of chia seeds

- 1 teaspoon of cinnamon powder
- 1 teaspoon of vanilla extract
- 4-5 ice cubes

Directions:

1. Wash and peel the carrots and apple, then chop them into small pieces.
2. In a blender, add the chopped carrots, apple, almond milk, chia seeds, cinnamon powder, and vanilla extract.
3. Blend the ingredients until they achieve a smooth and creamy consistency.
4. Add the ice cubes and blend again until the mixture is chilled.
5. Transfer the smoothie into a glass and serve promptly.

Nutritional information per serving:

- Calories: 115
- Carbohydrates: 21g
- Fiber: 8g
- Protein: 2g

- Fat: 3g
- Sodium: 99mg

39. Strawberry Banana Smoothie

Preparation Time: 5 minutes

Yield: 2 servings

Ingredients:

- 1 medium banana, peeled and sliced
- 1 cup frozen strawberries
- 1 cup unsweetened almond milk
- 1/2 cup plain Greek yogurt
- 1 tsp vanilla extract
- 1 tsp honey (optional)

Directions:

1. Add all ingredients to a blender.
2. Process on high speed until the mixture becomes smooth and creamy.
3. Taste and add honey if desired.

4. Pour into a glass and enjoy!

Nutritional Information per Serving:

- Calories: 140
- Total Fat: 3g
- Cholesterol: 5mg
- Sodium: 90mg
- Total Carbohydrates: 25g
- Dietary Fiber: 3g
- Sugars: 14g
- Protein: 7g

40. Green Keto Smoothie with Avocado and Peanut Butter

Ingredients:

- 1 ripe avocado
- 1 cup of unsweetened almond milk
- 1 cup of fresh spinach
- 1 tablespoon of peanut butter
- 1/2 teaspoon of vanilla extract
- 1/2 teaspoon of stevia or any other low-calorie sweetener
- 1/2 cup of ice cubes

Directions:

1. Begin by halving the avocado and extracting the pit. Transfer the creamy flesh into a blender.
2. Add the almond milk, spinach, peanut butter, vanilla extract, and stevia to the blender.
3. Process on high speed until the mixture becomes smooth and creamy.
4. Add the ice cubes and blend again until the smoothie reaches a desired consistency.

5. Transfer the smoothie into a glass and serve promptly.

Nutritional information per serving:

- Calories: 205
- Total Fat: 18g
- Saturated Fat: 2.5g
- Sodium: 155mg
- Total Carbohydrates: 9g
- Dietary Fiber: 6g
- Sugars: 1g
- Protein: 5g

Conclusion

This diabetic smoothie recipe book provides an excellent resource for individuals who want to manage their diabetes while enjoying delicious and healthy smoothies. The recipes in this book use nutritious ingredients and are designed to help regulate blood sugar levels.

By incorporating these smoothies into a healthy diet and lifestyle, individuals with diabetes can improve their overall health and well-being. Additionally, the recipes are easy to prepare and can be adapted to suit individual preferences.

Made in United States
Troutdale, OR
11/27/2024